Picking Wild Raspberries
The Imaginary Love Poems of Gertrude Stein

ROSEMARY AUBERT

Rosemary Aubern

*To Eve and Donald
with best wishes*

Rosemary

Sono Nis Press
Victoria   British Columbia   1997

Canadian Cataloguing in Publication Data

Aubert, Rosemary
  Picking Wild Raspberries
  ISBN 1-55039-075-9
  1. Stein, Gertrude, 1874-1946 - Poetry. I. Title.
PS8551.U24P52 1997   C811'.54   C97-910666-4
PR9199.3.A9P52 1997

We acknowledge the support of the Canada Council for
the Arts for our publishing program.

Cover art by Phyllis Serota
Design by Annie Weeks

Published by Sono Nis Press
1725 Blanshard Street
Victoria, British Columbia
Canada V8W 2J8

Printed and bound in Canada by Morriss Printing Company Ltd.
Victoria, British Columbia

This book is dedicated to
my friend and colleague
Pat Jasper
in appreciation for her expertise,
kindness, and encouragement.

Poems in this collection have appeared in
An Invisible Accordion, *Contemporary Verse 2*,
Canadian Literature, and *The Fiddlehead*.

Contents

Picking Wild Raspberries

At first I couldn't believe my eyes
that among all the dull green leaves
and the brambles
there should suddenly be
anything that red.

Immediately my mouth
began to long for
the sweet/tart fruit.

But I warned myself away.
What if the bushes concealed
    a snake?
    a small biting mammal?
    a bog?
    a patch of poison weed?

Just one.
I promised myself just one
and I reached and touched
and it fell into my palm
with the ease of fate.

Of course after the first
red burst of it on my tongue
there had to be more—
so I reached again and again
until I was following
the little red lanterns
deep into the bush.

By then, oblivious to insects
and slippery stones
and even the cry of hungry birds
I just kept going and grabbing
and my only fear
was that somehow the rich berries
might fall from my hands
before they could reach my open mouth.

I never stopped
until I'd eaten every one in sight.

Later, I thought
there was nothing else
like a wild red raspberry:
the sighting, the reaching
the abandonment to risk
the succulent reward.

I thought there was nothing else in the world
like that.

But of course, there is.

Alice In A Spanish Shawl Rides Bareback Along The Seacoast Toward Tres Pinos

It was before me, but still
I liked to think of you
riding madly beside the sea,
your horse as wild as yourself.

You rode away from the old men
the grandfathers, brothers, uncles—
whatever they all were—
rode away from your prim gray dresses
and solid shoes
and purses that snapped like a slap.

Maybe it was dawn,
the California beach pink and smooth as skin
beneath the hooves of the horse
black fringe flying
the mane, the shawl, your hair.…

Maybe the waves roared a secret
you dared not hear.
Maybe your trapped heart
lifted and soared anyway.

Then you went back home
to the old men and their boiled dinners.

After, as you sat on the tidy verandah
and felt the wind blow gently up from where
the sea grew quiet in the dusk,
the secret scented the breeze and teased your ear.

It was before me
and I am no oracle
who can send messages all around the world
and into your ear.
At least, I wasn't then.

But I always loved to think of you
sitting there,
an unnamed joy
loosening the reins of your maiden heart.

To May Bookstaver

I didn't know at first
what it was about you.

I thought it was the light—
the way it seemed to fall
across your face
making you look like a painting
though that was before I loved the paintings.

Then I thought it might be your perfume
the scent of flowers caught
under a late spring snow.

Then I thought it must be your laugh
that crooked, catchy melody.
But listen, May,
I knew you were laughing at me.
I was foolish but never fooled.

Though I certainly didn't know at first
why
when I was with you
I was me
and also somebody not me
wanting something but not knowing what.

Then one afternoon,
I walked away from your room
leaving behind a book
and you ran after me.

I almost didn't wait.
I almost ran away.
Because your footfall in the hall
hit inside me
like the pound of a drum in a parade.

My ears
my throat
my chest
my stomach pounding
and then the pounding
between my thighs.

I just stood there, shocked
by my desire for you.

You rounded the corner and caught me
staring, my mouth open
my hands clenched helplessly at my side,
a silly virgin, a stupid voyeur.

And you ran up to me
and into me
and started to laugh
and have been laughing ever since.

I hear the tune of it sometimes
a mean bird singing
in the lovely trees.

Alice At The Spring Salon

I came up behind where you sat with a friend,
two small women
in front of two big paintings:
the prim in front of the wild—
no, the apparently prim
in front of the apparently wild.
And of course I burst out laughing.

You turned, and your great black eyes
showed shock,
soon softening into pleasure,
though you couldn't know
that I saw that
and had to laugh again.

The *vernissage* swirled around us,
the *vrai vie de Bohème* as you liked to say.
And the long low building
thrown up like a tent in the park
glowed with the light of Paris and spring.

"What do you think, Miss Toklas?" I teased you.
And I watched your mouth as you answered.
Later I remembered the mouth, but not the answer.

She is like these paintings, I thought
*trapped in rectangles and squares
and ready to explode.*
I laughed again and left you
with your surprise and your little friend.

But all I could think of all afternoon
was ways to see you again.
It was hard, distracted as I was,
by the *vernissage*.

Finally, it hit me.
I remembered Picasso's Fernande
and how she needed students of French
to pay the rent.

"Miss Toklas," I said
coming up behind you again
and putting my hand on your shoulder.
You jumped.
"You must start to learn French at once.
I've found you a teacher already.
Will you come?"

I watched your mouth as you answered.
I remember the mouth, but not the answer,
though of course it must have been "Yes."

The Little Note

Pussy, you told everybody
about the *petit bleu*
the little note you sent
to say you'd be delayed
for our first date.

You told everybody how I stood there
holding it and saying, "It is over."

Then you told everybody:
"I didn't know what had happened.
She was very different from the day before—
She was a vengeful goddess; I was afraid."

But I will tell them
how it really was
and what happened
and why I wasn't laughing
when I opened the door
to find you standing in the sunshine
on the *rue de Fleurus*.

That morning, I had awakened
thinking of your dark hair—
how it swept along your brow
dipped to hide the space above your eyes.
Already I was looking into your eyes.

From my window, I heard Paris coming awake
the clop of the vendor's mule on the cobblestones
the children in their colored ribbons peeping to school
the rising pigeons cooing in the eaves.

And I tried to hear your voice again in my mind.
But you had been so quiet
watching me, listening to me—
that nothing came into the silence I was making for you
but the sound of the street waking up.

So I rose and took coffee and walked to the window
and looked out over all the city.
Somewhere, I said to myself,
she is rising and dressing and coming to me.

More coffee
and baguettes that the baker's boy
had left by the door.
And I thought: Slim as she is,
somewhere she breakfasts and thinks:
By dinner Miss Stein and I will be friends.

More coffee.
I dressed, the roughness of my clothes
making me think of the silkiness of yours.
Somewhere, I said to the air,
She adjusts her collar, straightens her hem.

A whole morning of this!

Then the bell and my heart jumping
like the pigeons at a sudden sound
or the leaves outside at the breeze.

When I read your *petit bleu*
my heart jumped again.
Not because it said you'd be late
but because it meant you were coming for sure.

And when you did come
and I saw you
and I said "It is over."
I never meant Us—
which was just about to begin.

All that was over
was how I'd been waiting
all of my previous life.

Italy: 1908 Alice Throws Her Red Corset Out The Window Of A Train

In the beginning—
our first trip to Italy,
when I decided, then
asked you to be my wife—
I used to watch you
all the time.

So small, so careful, so dark
compared, of course, to me.

I noticed you ate the way birds eat
not the cliché
but the care
this, not this, this, not, not
a berry is a not a nut,
is it, Pussy?

And how you sat
edge of the seat
if the floor was prepared to meet you
feet tucked under otherwise.

Perfect purse, perfect hat.
Later you would teach me
about purses and hats.
But in the pictures of Italy
mine are baskets and barrels
yours are tassels and silk.

At night,
though you never knew it
I woke up sometimes
to listen to you breathe
regular a clock
a calendar
the rhythm of the train
to Florence
when we went
as two ladies travelling.
Then you skipped a breath
and my heart skipped a beat.

I figured out
everytime she'll do that
I'll be scared
and want her more.

But there you were again sleeping
regular a clock
a calendar
the rhythm of the train
to Florence.

In the morning you said it was
too hot to wear any clothes at all,
disappeared toward the other end
of the railroad car.

Next thing I knew
your red corset
went flying past my face
outside the window
and into the hills of Italy.

My heart skipped a beat.

Your underwear all of a sudden
a candle in the wind
a small flame made great.

Okay, I decided
I love her for it
and I love you for it.

Mabel At The Table

Then there was the day you got mad
over lunch at Mabel Dodge.

One of those golden days
country leaves crisp as a pie.
French breeze cools the soup.
I'm sitting in her husband Edwin's chair
across from her
and she looks up.

All I did was not turn away
all I did was let the light arc
like Edison
all I did was look and see
how beautiful she was.
How beautiful she was:
when I smiled at her,
it was as though I were looking
in a mirror for the first time
and I always like what I see
in a mirror.

But you, sparrow, you bird, you Alice
jumped up like a popped chestnut
whosh out the door onto the terrace
your brown dress just another one of
those leaves.

How could you be hurt by just a look?
Is that a word? Is that a touch or
some kind of promise? No.
Well, listen, I *did* promise didn't I?
Never to do it again
never ever do it
never
never again
never ever again, little Alice
never again until next time.

Alice Typing

Before you came to live with me
you came to type.

I would still be sleeping
after a long night of work.
I'd rise, walk out
and there you'd be
behind the Smith-Premier
like an elegant elf behind a hill.

I came to know
that your fingers were more strong than swift
but I didn't know at first
what a good thing that can be.

After only a little while,
you were helping me
with the writing, too,
helping me figure out
all the kinds of ones there are.

One day, I said your kind:
"an old-maid mermaid."
I said it to make you laugh
but you didn't.
Instead, I saw quick tears
which you pretended not to shed
and I pretended not to see.

Your strong fingers, though,
quickened on the keys
and I knew then
how they would feel
on my skin
and in my hair
and I drew in a sharp breath
which I pretended not to draw
and you pretended not to hear.

Later, but not much later,
it became clear to us both
that you were more mermaid
than old maid.

We picked buttercups and hyacinths,
forget-me-nots and miguets.
I wove a wreath of wild violets
for your hair
your long black, sea-swept hair.

To Alice

I hold up to your lips
these brown apples
these russet apples of late fall
I hold up to your lips
these soft hands kept white
by the work of your own
I hold up to your lips
this day and how it starts
with you wakening first
to watch me wake
I hold up to your lips
all our secrets not only
how we are such ladies
but also how we are not
I hold up to your lips
your silk things so many so smooth
and also my rough clothes my rough
laughing self
I hold up to your lips
our America far away and perfect
I hold up to your lips
the America between my thighs
that is our kingdom Alice isn't it?
It'll be a long time before anybody
talks about that
but I hold it up to your lips
now.

Alice In Spain

You said, and you were right
that in Granada I first felt
"a desire to express the rhythm
 of the visible world."

"No greater tragedy than to be
born blind in Granada,"
the Spanish say.
They're right, too.

And so I wrote of the visible rhythm of you
in your Spanish disguise:
    Black silk coat.
    Black gloves.
    Black fan.
    Black hat with its single vibrant flower.

In Granada that first summer
you were a shadow
moving into and out of arches of light:
a Moor disengaged from her Moordom.

Watching you dance with joy
among the white pillars of the Alhambra
I felt words fail me.
But it was a good failure,
as if never again
would I be owned by what I said
by anything, really.

In Cuenca
I bought a rhinestone turtle.
The curious villagers
followed us to see
it and you.

In Avila
you threatened to stay Spanish forever.
I panicked and flew into
my one and only rage,
came close to losing you.

It was then that I learned
what I must have:
words set free from the jail of words
a heart set free from the absence of you.

For the rest of the trip
and my life
I had both.

Alice And I One Summer

We are in Italy—or perhaps it is Spain.
Anyway, it is certainly summer.

Alice, who hates the heat
is sitting underneath a tree weeping.

Several Spanish—or Italian—birds
have been silenced by this sound
so all around us
except for the weeping
the countryside is still
and we are at peace.

I am lying on my back in a meadow
with my face toward the sun.
There is a trick to looking
straight into the sun
with your eyes wide open.
Nobody knows it but me.

The light scorches me clean.
I feel my vision become a liquid
in which the landscape can float without weight.
My neck is a rod made pliable
in the iron-furnace.
I can bend it almost without moving—
toward and away from the searing rays.
Even my head is hot and loose and so free
that it seems to move like a planet
around and around
the burning sun.

If I could, I would lie like this forever
this melted and lax and free.

This safe,
knowing that should I start to singe,
there would come Alice
with all her tears
to put my fire out.

To Alice, Also

You are my dark
my small, exquisite shadow.

When I stand in our garden,
it is you between me and the earth
shielding our roses from my heat.

You are the dusk
into which I hurry
after the long light of our busy days.

Before you—
I can't really remember before you—
but if I could I would think
how dazzling everything was
how there was no pause
for the heart or the hand or the eye.

Now, however, I turn
and there you are:
my shade, my evening, my rest.

Beyond the walls of Bilignin, Alice
I hear the nightbirds begin
their solemn song.

But there is no sadness here.
I reach out and gather about me
you, my most excellent night.

A Day In The Country

This morning, Alice, when we had
the pale bananas and the bananas
and the pale rose on the banana plate,
I thought of writing of the cow.

Now that we are here
among the grass and the blades of grass
among grass and the grassy mounds
among the sky and the fields where the cow
pursues the grass and the grass is passive
beneath the cow: now we will write.
Not I, not you, but you and I.

A cow is a cow is
the afternoon, the field, us,
what we do and what we don't do
what we have decided
and what we have decided not to do.

Alice, chase the cow toward the fence,
which encloses all that it encloses
and excludes all that it cannot enclose.
Chase the cow before my eyes, before the hand
that holds the pen.

And again.

We are, you and I, two hands:
the hand that holds the pen
the hand that holds the stick;
we are two separate hands, yet a pair
that is us.
You and I, the seer and the seen,
two ladies with a cow in a field
two geniuses—

I, of course,
am the right hand one.

I Am

I am the love of your life.
I'm the treasure chest with its one big
and many little jewels
also the one good cup of tea.

I'm that morning in August when
the hot sun loses its grip
and autumn leaps round the corner
frisky as a pup
jumps into your skinny arms, Alice.

I am a cigar when you dare to smoke one
and a fast kiss behind
the shelves of Sylvia Beach's bookstore.

I am how twilight blows its blue breath
over the rough edges of day and
invites our nights—still sweet,
still such a surprise—to come in, okay, come in now.

I am, as you have always said, a Sousa band
blaring on Main Street
down which, you, following me
march boldly, your little feet cool in my shadow.

I am the love of your life,
a huge butterfly laughing at
the startled face peering into your net.
You've caught me, yes, you clever little Alice
and I will not stray.

I am the love of your life.
And I owe you.

My Jew

I called you that because you were.

Others said you were a gypsy
with your dark, demanding eyes
your midnight hair
your face like a chiselled statue
of some strange obsidian—
pale for obsidian
but darker than anything else.

You were not a gypsy
                a Moor
                a Spaniard
                a Cleopatra
                    removed from the Nile.

You were a Jew
and I was too.

I loved that about us
even though I toyed with saints
and you came to pray to them
in a way reserved for nuns.

You were not a nun
not even at the end.

I called you my Jew
because
to be what we were was a bond to me
and a wall.
We lived, you and I
in a ghetto, a pale
a cabal of love
a club
whose members numbered only two:

Me and my Jew.

In This Church, My Body

In this church, my body,
I worship you: my wife.

It will be a long time before
there are churches for
people like you and me
even in Paris the City of Churches
(not that I'd go anyway)
so you and I, Alice
are on our own.

In this church, my body,
I feel the pulse of your body
an organ, the peal of bells.
May the world, when it remembers us
remember this:
that a faithful wife is a blessing
to the end of days.

At the end of our days,
each of them,
there you always were
sitting on your little stool
your sewing in your hand.

If it were summer,
there'd be sun still
and raspberry cordial to drink.
In winter: the false fire
and *chocolat*.
Then bed, warm and safe.

A faithful wife is a blessing beyond count.
In this church, my body
I count my thousands of days with you,
the way a nun counts her beads,
the way *you* counted yours,
praying that we would meet in heaven.

Did we?

The Continuous Present As A Cake

Natalie Barney once said
that Alice and I in search of cakes
were like two miners
in search of a perfect jewel
and this is true.

One lives in Paris for a number of reasons
and cakes is one of the reasons.

I remember especially
a small *pâtisserie*
on the edge of the *Place des Vosges*.
Here, one warm autumn day,
Alice and I discovered a *gâteau aux prunes*
so delectable
that we sat right down and ate it on the spot
among sweepers, pigeons and fallen leaves.

Alice, of course, ate like a bird
even when eating cake.
How it pleased me to watch her—
no crumbs ever losing their place
to skitter and slide into her lace.

I would, now that all is over,
give heaven for a bite of cake
and the sight of Alice eating it.

But cakes are for time
and mine is gone.

Pussy Dusts A Picasso

Art appreciation:
the softest rag, no polish, no water, no lint
no pressure.

On your toes, a ladder, a chair, a breath
you balance, Pussy, as if
you too are part of
the composition.

Dark head against green face
dark face against the yellow eye
slim bend of Alice and of paint
not one, one, not.

Sometimes I think Pablo left a space
where you, your apron, your rag and
your care
slip in to make it whole.

Once you said
nobody knows these paintings like I do
and it's true.

Closeup you know them
like a bird knows the chimney pots
like a bird knows that little piece of Paris
and from that piece
knows also
all the rest.

After Sitting For The Picasso Portrait

There were these many afternoons
that I spent sitting
under the great black eyes
not daring to move
or even to breathe
until I just couldn't wait anymore.

Afterwards, exhaled from his studio,
I would walk down
from Montmartre to Montparnasse
watching the sun get tangled
in the chestnut trees
before it sank from sight.

Stalking the darkening neighborhoods
I took the city street by street
the way a rich man samples the girls—

In the little cafés the waiters snapped
fresh white linen
over the bare tables of afternoon
changing the hour from apéritif to dinner.

In front of the picture galleries
the dealers drew in their wares
like a housewife draws
her line of many-colored dresses
out of the wind and the sun
and into the still of the house.

Walked and walked and walked.

At the bridge I stopped and watched
the opening eyes of the lamps
blink back from the river
the buildings
the street.
Paris, city of light.

I hurried then, toward Alice and home
working as I went
on my sentences,
letting my feet measure out
the rhythm of my words.
"A rose is a rose is a rose…."

Everything flowed perfectly then:
the words, the river, the night,
the knowing
of the great dark eyes that I left
and the great dark eyes I sped toward.

I embraced the whole city.
At the bottom of it all
I felt
a great heart pounding.

Was it the heart of Paris?
Or was it me?

To My Ex-friend May Bookstaver

For years your name was an enemy
lying in ambush
a single syllable
carrying a gun,
a crook in the shadows
between two buildings
waiting to jump out
into the light of the streetlamps
eager to steal
the very thing
I finally thought was safe.

"Do you hear from May?"
someone would ask.
And there I lay
shot dead.

For years your name
escaped from the prison
of my resolve,
scaled walls,
studied smuggled maps
just to find a good road
back to me.
Friends harbored it
like a fugitive.

For years your name
was like the warden's bell
before sleep.
One peal and I'd rest lightly, if at all.

Then one morning,
Alice turned to me and said,
"You remember May?"

"Last month?"

"No, Lovey," she laughed,
"Not the month—the girl—"

Your name!
I captured it on my tongue
kept it in the cell of my mouth
waited, then set it free.

"May."

Nothing.

For years your name
seemed a life sentence.

Now it was like any other name.
Nothing but a word.

Parole.

Gertrude Stein At The Wheel

I loved the way the steering wheel
felt between my hands
round and hard and smooth
like a coin
or a pie pan
or dish made from Italian clay.

I loved how the trees whizzed by
so fast their leaves became one leaf
just the way Picasso painted them.

I loved looking up at the sky
the mountains
the meadows
the fields—
driving is like a museum.

And I loved the road itself:
how it curled in front of me like a sleeping dog,
never telling me where it was going
til we got there.

Also I loved
how when something broke down
somebody could be talked into
fixing it.

And of course
I loved how Alice
would hang onto her hat,
her white, clutching fingers
the only still thing
in the landscape that whirled and flew
and threw itself at me
everywhere I looked.

Pussy In The Homicide Car: Chicago 1935

The night is a great big O
Oh Pussy, look at you!
Your eyes are great big O's.

We slide through the scary streets
the homicide car like a big knife
juliennes the night.

We are famous now, and brave
in fact if I were at the wheel
we'd go faster
any gangster too slow off his feet
smash.

O, Alice, O such great big eyes
such a lady, with your tiny purse.
Pussy, Don't be afraid, I'm here

Black, white, black
shadow, shadow and light.
We're a movie now, aren't we, Alice?
flicking into and out of these streets.

In every doorway lurks
What?
A shadow of a shadow of a shadow.
Guns breathe down our necks,
the hair there standing on end.

Nobody says it, do they Alice
that we—you and I—
are outlaws, too?
on the lam from the soft salon
from the Paris mornings
sweet among the chestnut trees.

The homicide car is lurching, speeding
that's the way!
Danger screams us around a corner.

I reach for your little hand
and hold it where cops can't see.

O, Pussy, O
my outlaw
my partner in delicate crime.

How Pussy Liked The Roosevelt Hotel

Very well very very well, thank you
that's how.

First of all it was America, New Orleans.
Pussy danced a jazz dance in our suite
thought nobody saw
but I did
and so did the maid
who laughed a deep black laugh
a jazz dance, too.

Then we ate jambalaya.
Pussy was shocked
everything mixed together like that
three kinds of meat in the same dish.
After she said, oh Baby, I'm full.
Never heard Alice be full before.

Red carpets she liked
crystal chandeliers
brass even, Pussy even liked the brass
though shiny things usually
put her out.

In the lobby linen shop
she bought handkerchieves
good strong American handkerchieves
unlike her Belgian lace, her Alençon.

But best she liked the jazzmen
thought I didn't know.
One night while I was writing
she snuck out.

I searched the tea shop
the newsstand
the door toward Canal Street.
Asked the doormen like soldiers
in their sharp red suits.
No.

Leaned in for a moment
at the lobby bar
where a saxophone wailed
like a Paris cat.

Went upstairs scared
I never lost Alice before.

Two hours later, she came back
smiling, tapping her little feet.

That night in the Roosevelt
I had a dream
that Pussy was drinking Bourbon
and playing the sax.

In the morning we breakfasted
dressed.
Pussy chose silk
and Alençon lace.

Alice Picking Strawberries At Bilignin

One morning at Bilignin
I awoke to see you
picking strawberries in our walled garden.
Though I had only begun my sleep,
you were already up and dressed.
Light blue silk, as befits a summer morning,
slid along your thigh
to show its curve
as you bent down.
I watched like a bird,
waited like a bird
for my sweet, fresh breakfast.
Beneath the curl of dark friendly leaves
close to the earth and warm as its touch,
your fingers surveyed the little plants
like a blind man reading the face of his lover.
You found two for the basket
and one for your lips.
I watched some more.
You raised a red berry
and delicately took it with the tip of your tongue.
"Alice is picking strawberries," I said to myself,
"before the sun kisses them
before I kiss her."

Your Hands

Your hands could knit while your eyes read.
Your hands embroidered Picasso and
made his paintings into covers for chairs.
Your hands baked good American apple pies.
Your hands on the Smith-Premier turned my scratch into books.
Your hands kept all our pictures clean.
And our cool bed smooth.
And our floor shiny underneath our feet.
At night your hands knew unspeakable secrets
and told them freely in the safety of our bed.
Your hands brushed our long tangled hair
until it flowed like the Seine—
then, on a whim, cut it off.
Your hands wrote menus and wine lists and orders and checks.
Your hands made music.
Your hands in the garden
teased our roses away from their thorns.
In the laundry, smacked linen until it cracked clean
then snapped it out into the sun to dry....
Your hands were the hands of my clock
and when it ran down
you lifted your fingers
and shut the lids of my eyes.
I was in your hands.
I always was.

Missing You

From here I can look at you, Pussy,
and I do.

I see that you are smaller still
than you ever were.

I see you smoking so many cigarettes
and wearing black clothes
made of stout material to last
as many seasons as they can.

I see you sitting in your single room
the feet that I kept warm
resting on a cheap electric fire.

I see what you eat now, Pussy.
Nothing—as compared to nearly nothing before.

I know that you are shivering and starving
to save my pictures.

Sell them, Pussy.
I loved Pablo but I loved you more
oh, much, much more.

And I see, too, don't think I don't
that you're a Catholic now.

I called you "My Jew" and you are
even from the first your thick dark hair
was the hair of Esther and of Ruth

Wither thou goest, Alice
I would still like to go
as I always did
from the day we met.

I also said
"When a Jew dies, he's dead."
I meant that there's no need for heaven.

But if there was and I was God
I'd pick for eternity
only the interesting people,
wouldn't you?

I'd pick you Alice
I picked you every time.

I don't know what's worse
to see you huddled beneath your only coat
in the apartment nobody visits
or to see you say your Catholic prayers
or to see you weep over my grave
even after all these years.

But listen, Pussy,
it's okay.

Time will be good to you and me
our pictures, our friends
Basket our dogs
our writings
our love
our lives.

Since the day we wed
nobody says my name
without saying yours.

Forever and ever.
Amen.

Mata Hari Dances Nude

Here's a mystery:
What does the eye see
when everything is right there in front of it
like a broad daylight window
looking over somebody's front yard?

Everybody said Mata Hari was a spy
that each of her many jewels
was an eye
that her voice was the voice of wireless messages
across the black-out sea.

Not me.

I dreamed of her
long after she galloped through Natalie Barney's garden,
her horse wearing more than she wore
—and even then only emeralds and pearls.

I dreamed she was talking to me
in some kind of code:
raised right arm (plump and perfect)
meant, "All is safe."
Bare thigh—"Beware!"
Neck arched above naked breast—
"An enemy is near...."

In the dream, I was naked, too.
Like a billboard, and it said,
"Gertrude, wake up!"

No. A spy cannot dance naked
and stay a spy.
In the light of day,
what is seen is what is seen.

On the other hand,
Alice is a spy.
I have caught her hovering,
her silky garments silenced in their swish.

She is watching me watch Mata Hari dance nude.
Try as she might to hide them, Alice reveals
state secrets: her black eyes emerald green.

A Poem To Miss Josephine Baker

Which begins: Thank you
for your Salomé dance of feathers
and for the strong brown line of
your perfect legs.

My fellow exile
sweet shadow
I wish I could touch you
are you sequin or satin
are you smooth or rough?

And your hair?
How does it feel to finger those strands
tousled by dance
or tamed by your helmet of diamond pavé?
Who runs their fingers through it,
or not daring to go that far
hovers like a curious servant
longing to unstopper the bottles of your rich perfume?

I like to think about you and the music
I am free to think as I like.
Like to think of you as if you were mine
as if I could write you or love you,
dear Miss Baker formerly of the USA

Listen, a Jew knows a few things
and I'm not blind.
There, what would we be, you and I?
A colored dancehall girl

riding in a Cadillac, sure
home to the worst part of town.
And I — somebody's fat sister who went to Harvard
so listens to hysterical, wealthy women
coddle their complaints…

But what are we here?
I a genius.
You the queen of ruffle, strut and light.

Which is good, then, isn't it?

Come a little closer, Josephine
let me feel your gown
your hand.

Let me run my mind along
all that lovely dark.

Legends, when they touch, touch nothing
except the news.

But let's pretend.
Pretend you are the genius and I am you.
Let me dance in your skin
Miss Baker
let me touch you
from the inside out
like a star touches
the inside of heaven
prick of light
penetrating black.

What I Told Sylvia Beach

I never really loved other people's books.
Oh, I didn't mind browsing in Shakespeare and Company
especially because it wasn't too dusty
and all the books were in English.

But nobody's book
ever made me feel
as good as my own.

As I used to say to Alice,
there are babies and there are babies,
but if it isn't *your* baby,
why bother?

Well, I had no babies,
only my own good books.
As I told Sylvia Beach,
If you're going to love anything,
love close.

Sherwood Anderson And His Wife Tennessee

There are a lot of wonderful things
in the writer world
but few are as good
as a struck-dumb admirer.

So when Sherwood came to Paris,
I needed it to be
just him and me.

Tennessee Anderson sat
perched upon a table,
her long American legs
crossed,
her little pink ears
like microphones.

I gave Alice our signal
and very nicely
she dragged Tennessee Anderson
kicking her long white legs
into the kitchen for tea.

Sherwood and me.

I said he was the only man in America
who could write a clear and passionate sentence.

Like this one:
"Gertrude, it was a vital day for me
when I stumbled upon you."

To Ernest Hemingway

While Alice is in the kitchen
making us lunch
let me look at you long and hard.

I like the looks of a strong young man
always have.
Used to like to look long and hard
at my brother Leo.
Used to love Leo like a brother
which he was, then wasn't, isn't, damn him.

Here's what I see in you:
the hunger.
For what?
For wildness
as if to tear open a sentence or a life
or an animal
could free something
and in its escape
free you.
For fame
which is my hunger, too
and for love,
the kind of love that you don't think
is love like Alice
but it is.

It's hard to see how a woman making you
lunch in the kitchen
could be
the same as fame, writing and the hunt
especially if it's Alice
so, you have to take my word,
which is, after all,
a little better than your word just yet.

To be a genius
when nobody but you
knows you're a genius
is a hard thing.
To hunt at home,
every room a lair is
also hard.

To be famous at home
is almost impossible
though not quite.
Not everybody understands this
but those who understand
write and bask and pounce when they can.
Ah, here's Alice.

One Of The Things I Told Ernest Hemingway

I said, "You can buy pictures or clothes.
Unless you're very rich, you can't buy both."

I chose a long brown robe
and several vibrant Picassos.
I chose a basket-top hat
and Cézanne.
I chose a loose belt made of rope
like a monk
and Matisse.

Once a child said of Alice and me,
"The woman is scary, but I like the man."
I was that man
in my plain brown robe.

Another time,
a whole Italian village bowed to me
because they thought
I was a bishop come to bless their crops.
So you see, clothes have their value, too.
I have heard that in New York
somebody paid two thousand dollars
for a pair of Alice's shoes—
which just goes to show you:
you can buy (even today)
Alice's clothes
or else you can buy paintings.

Take your pick.

Another Thing I Told Ernest Hemingway

One cold day he came into the warmth
of the studio, sat down and started to tell me
how as a boy in Kansas City
he had to run from the wolves:
not animals,
but the railroad tramps who went after little boys
to rape them.

And Hemingway,
who was always in love with violent death
said, "If they know you can kill them,
they sense it and let you alone."

I, of course, wanted to teach him
tolerance, and pity, even
for those whose lives are repugnant.
But a silence came into things,
and I failed.

All I ended up saying
was that women who sleep with women
do things that aren't repugnant
and afterwards are happy
and lead very lady-like lives.

Hemingway just shrugged.
Later he went home
and made rough love to his wife.

Picasso And Me

A genius wakes up one day
even as a baby and already knows
that the world is waiting
in its impatient way.

A genius is always alone
even in the same room with
another genius
and words
are not what geniuses say to each other.

Also, a genius sits on top of history
and feels it
all the time shifting
like a chair with three legs.

But it is not yesterday
that geniuses think about.
Geniuses have to figure out
how today is going to
get to be tomorrow.

I was never kidding
and I am not now.
No matter what we might have been
to each other,
Picasso and I were geniuses to the world
and we can prove it.

After him
nobody looked at painting
the same way again.

And after me...
Well—
everything but me
came after me.

Bravig Imbs

Was one of the pleasant young men
I liked to keep around
    like a clean handkerchief
    or an extra bottle of wine.

The first time he came
I was watching out the window.
Of course I noticed how handsome he was.

Though Bravig Imbs
    was dressed as a banker:
        Blue suit.
        White shirt.
        Blue tie.
        Black shoes.

How quaint he is, I said to myself,
Did he come to offer a loan?

At the door
he stopped suddenly, looked up
the way Basket used to look up
at a bigger dog in the street.

I ducked behind the curtain
but not before I saw Bravig Imbs
surreptiously slip from his wrist
a thin circle of glass
a crystal bracelet that
caught the light of the sun.

Alice had told me a long time before
that rings and bracelets are links of a chain
binding lovers and friends.

I realized at once
that the pleasant young man
had worn that crystal link
to prove to us
that he wasn't a banker after all.

His lack of courage on the step
didn't count.
I smiled at Bravig Imbs.
I let him in.
And every time he opened his handsome mouth that day,
I encouraged him.
Because all the time he was there
I could feel
the crystal link in the cave of his pocket
growing into a chain.

Several Men Named Francis

A man named Francis is always just coming from
a place of miracles
or always just about to go to one.
I have known several men named Francis
and this is always true.

Once I listened to Picabia talk about genius
all afternoon.
At four—it was winter and the sun was thinking about setting—
he stood up and said,
"All of Paris is one blue line quivering."
Then he went out into the street
and it was.

Francis Rose was like that, too,
born as he was
in the middle of a thunderstorm
and surrounding himself
with the perfume of tar.

And of course, there was Of Assisi
who could speak to animals,
including our Basket, I guess.

I said that all men named Francis
are "very beautiful to hear, to see and to do."

And as Of Assisi might have said to my dog,
"Gertrude, of course, is correct."

Why I Loved To Buy Paintings

I know what people think
now that I'm gone
and Cézanne goes
for millions:
"Shrewd old Jew, she knew
plant a penny, reap a pound."

And I knew what Alice thought:
that I bought paintings
just to meet the painters,
young men with beautiful eyes
and wives that sat in the kitchen with her.

And I know what Leo my brother thought:
that buying paintings would make us Parisians
instead of the good Americans
we really were.

It wasn't for that
or even for color or shape
or the sight of them displayed on the wall
like the shields of warriors
fighting their way
into the twentieth century.

No. I bought paintings
because of the stillness:
A man leans on a hoe
and all around him
the world stops:
the fields lie fallow
the clouds hang poised
his hair, though lifted by wind
won't move.

Later, the stillness was
the breath between two thoughts,
the breath one takes in shock
to see yellow beside such naked green.

But don't get me wrong,
I liked the money part, too,
how I could reach into my purse
and just pull out enough to buy
that moment
in which winter sun falls on the shoulder of a woman
and warms it
and always will.

Museum Windows

To look out a window
after looking all day at paintings
is like listening to a flute and a bird
on the same afternoon.

A painting holds the world
in a loose hand—
color spilling away from its object:
red leaking out of an apple
silver smudging the moon.

A line in a painting is a moving line
only if the eye moves
only if the eye is tricked by desire
into following wherever the line might lead.
It pretends to lead out of the painting
and toward the world
but really, like a maze
it leads back in.

A window, on the other hand
doesn't hold the world at all.
Outside the museum in the Paris street,
a little boy scoots by
bouncing a red rubber ball.

For a moment it seems an apple
a sun
a blot
a blob of red paint.

No, it is only a ball.

All around the Louvre
life goes on
which is life.

But to tell the truth,
windows make me dizzy
with how everything in them
is always running around.

My eye, moved by desire
looks again at the picture
the pulsing red of still paint.
The sure song of the flute
the same tomorrow
as now.

My Brother Leo

I loved Leo like a brother
all the time he was
which wasn't always
but that's life.

In the beginning
there was hardly me without him.
When our mother died
and our father
Leo and I were our mother and father
and that was fine.

When we went to school
I didn't feel like it
if Leo wasn't there.
Even Harvard
Even Johns Hopkins.

So I came to Paris
and we were us again
in the *rue de Fleurus*
with its pavillion
and its studio.
We bought the paintings
and began to be important and happy,
or so I thought.

But Leo,
who always wanted to be somebody,
always ended up being Leo instead.

The end of Leo, of course,
was Alice.
Not at first,
when he got her to type
his little writings,
but after
when I started to love her
instead of him.

Leo got mad and went
and a long time passed.

Years later, I saw him
in the street.
I bowed,
he raised his hat.
We moved on.

"Who was that gentleman?"
Alice asked.

"Leo," I said,
but it was already
long done.

I don't remember
if I ever saw him again.

The Warm Dark

Out of the warm dark come all good things.
Out of the womb came you, Alice
long enough ago, but still…
Out of the warm dark soil of your garden
turnips and carrots, dahlias and roses.
Out of the mouths of Negroes comes that laughter.
Out of the well of the pen warm from my hand: these words.
Out of the nights of August come the pleasures of our bed,
Out of the oven the bread, the pie, the *pain au chocolat*.
Mabel steps out of her black sable coat.
The Ford car's engine roars us onto the road.
Out of the warm night of spring comes summer.
Out of the warm night of spring comes morning.
Out of night comes morning
a little child creeping into day
and through
and toward
the warm dark that I love.

The Laughter of Negroes

I always loved the laughter of Negroes,
how sunshine it was
how full of sunshine
as if all warmth was nestled there
like a loaf of bread
in a basket.
In Negro laughter was our South
shaded afternoons of somebody else's rest,
magnolias of hidden regret.
I heard it first, though
in the streets of Baltimore
drifting around the shanty corner
and tapping me on the shoulder
so that I turned
and caught it, like a breath.
Over the years I learned
that the world of the Negro is secret
a mansion of sweetness and sorrow
hedged high from the eyes of whites.
But every fence has a gate.
Which is why
I always loved the laughter of Negroes
opening and letting me in.

Loving Laughing

Is to always listen and watch
for the possibility of it
and when it comes, like lightning,
to stand there and be struck.

Which sounds like it hurts
but it never does.

Is to let it start wherever it wants
in the mouth like a little song
or a sip of champagne.

In the throat
like brandy
warm and spreading
both up and down.

In the lungs
in the deep
well of the gut.

Loving laughing
is letting it
roll up and over
and go wherever it goes:
a long slide
down a fall of rough water,
a fast turn
in a hard-curved road.

Loving laughing is
throwing back your head
opening your mouth
and letting the eagle
fly over the thunderhead
into the sun.

Dear Professor James

I was a girl then, wasn't I?
Hard to think of me that way now
new and unsure even.
I haven't been since.

Here's my book,
write me a letter and tell me
what you think.

What I think is
I never would have done much
without you.
Tell you why.
It's hard when you're this smart
to look up.
Same as if you're tall,
which, as you know,
I'm not.

Once I asked myself
(girl that I was)
"Why is life worth living?"
And you were the answer.

Listening to you at Harvard
was like finding a big window in
a little wall.
I looked out and there was a world
during the day.
At night, a reflection
shot back a picture of you and me.
You teaching me.

The best thing is, Professor James,
as usual,
the simplest.
You were smart and you thought
I was smart, too.
That's lasted me
all these years.

Read this book
and let me know.
I'm waiting for a word from you
just like in the old days.

Any word especially a good one.

Thanks.
Your student,
Miss Stein.

Detective Novels

But I did love detective novels
because of how in them
there were three types of being:

Being the dead one.
Being the one who caused the dead one to be dead.
Being the one who caused the dead one to be dead to be caught.

Being the dead one
was often from being
one nobody very much wanted to be
a living one.
Which was good because
otherwise detective novels
would be greater tragedies
than they already are.

Being the one who caused the dead one to be dead
was sometimes being one who was brave
and sometimes being one who was greedy
and sometimes being one who loved but
couldn't have or be or keep
the one who was loved
and so caused them to be
the one that was dead.

To kill for love in detective stories,
is better than for money because
it is more poignant for causing
the one to be dead to be dead—
but not too much love
or else you have tragedy again.

I loved best to read about
the one who caused the one who caused the one to be dead to be
    caught
because that was almost always
the one with the guns and the car,
the one that chased the other one
from shadow to shadow
then caught him
and turned him in
and had a cigarette and a scotch,
then, when rested,
was ready for the next case
and the next one who would be the dead one.

But not too soon because
after all
even a fast reader like me
can't be one who is reading
all this too fast.

Or else it wouldn't be
tragedy enough.

I Didn't Live In America

Because I wanted America to live in me
and, of course, it does.

During the First World War
I sat at the bedside of doughboys
and read them the story
of the *Trail of the Lonesome Pine*.
I was that tree, really.
To be an American
not living in America
is always to be lonesome
—to be alone with yourself,
which is hard but
strong and good.

And there was also
I have to admit
Alice.
I did not ever
explain Alice to anyone
but in America
I would always have been thinking
how I could not.

Also, English.
Nobody around me could speak it
or read what I wrote.
So all of it was mine
only mine
like a secret code.
In America
everybody is always reading and understanding everybody.

Now look,
I don't ever mean to say
that I didn't love America.
I did
of course I always did.
During the Second World War
hiding away in the country in France
I waited in a cloud of mosquitoes
nearly all night long
just to see a car
of American officers pass.

America away from America
is perfect, precious and rare.

Whereas America in America
is just everywhere.

Simplicity

In the end you come to understand
that all things are one thing.

The rich pâtisserie becomes
the baker with his loaf of bread,
our wine cellar distills
the single glass of cloudless red.

In the end, not Bilignin
with its wild joy.
Instead, a small white camelia
worn on Alice's lapel.

Not paintings with their violent riot
and noisy rebellion.
Instead, a black line on the white page.

In the end you come to understand
it was not artists who held you.
It was art.
Not lovers, but love.
Not even Paris, with its fine display.
In the end it is only this room.

I said finally, "What is the question?"
Making everyone laugh as I died.

But I wasn't kidding.
In the end, there is no question.
Is is is.
It's as simple as that.